About

Bregita Basterfield is a bubbly and enthusiastic young woman residing in the bustling (and some say scary) city of Johannesburg, South Africa.

She started her writing career as a teenager and has added to her memoirs over the years. She holds a BBA Degree in marketing communication and a Post Graduate Certificate in education but her love lies in communication with people from all walks of life. She heads up a social leadership program and loves the idea of changing and improving people's lives one day at a time.

She is an adventure seeker and explorer and has revelled in climbing the Himalayas, walking the Camino and hiking for a good coffee spot. She lived in Israel and the UK for a few years and over the course of her life has travelled many parts of the world. She is a motivator, influencer and encourager. She has always loved song writing and poetry writing, and finds confidence and solace in words. She is a cheerleader for the masses and a peace maker.

She loves the idea that words can bring hope, bring comfort and bring a sense of reality; the idea that we all have struggles, all have dreams and all have realities that we both show the world and hide deep inside.

She is excited to bring these feeling and experiences to the world and let the world know, as unique as we all are, we need to lean on our similarities to keep strong and keep our heads held high. She recognises that her life could have turned out very different, but through Jesus she was rescued and now has the opportunity to tell her testimony and show the world that without Jesus, life has no meaning.

CONFIDENCE THROUGH OTHER MEASURES

BREGITA BASTERFIELD

CONFIDENCE THROUGH OTHER MEASURES

Vanguard Press

A CIP catalogue record for this title is
available from the British Library.

ISBN 978 1 80016 409 3

*Vanguard Press is an imprint of
Pegasus Elliot Mackenzie Publishers Ltd.*
www.pegasuspublishers.com

First Published in 2022

**Vanguard Press
Sheraton House Castle Park
Cambridge England**

Printed & Bound in Great Britain

Dedication

To the ones I love and the ones that love me

Acknowledgements

I want to thank all my family and friends. You have made me who I am today, and without you I wouldn't be half the person I am.

To Jesus — for rescuing me and for giving me the opportunity to tell my testimony and show the world that without you, life has no meaning. "For you created my inmost being; you knit me together in my mother's womb. I praise you because I am fearfully and wonderfully made; your works are wonderful I know that full well". *Psalms 139:13–16 NIV Bible*

Contents

Fairy dreams

The broken heart cannot bend
The crushed soul cannot mend
The runaway part cannot hide
The ringed finger cannot abide
The wholesome touch cannot feel
The dreamy sunset isn't real
The single one cannot tell
The craving love cannot yell
The stretched out hand cannot touch
And whisper softly, I love you much

Shooting star

Shooting star fall next to me

As I look up to the heavens I can see your face so clear
I remember the moments spent with you last year
Your loving touch held me from harm
Your presence still keeps me safe and warm
The careless nights spent by the flames
The lonely days now full of pain

So I sit and wonder can you hear my voice
Yeah I sit and wonder do I have a choice
You changed my life from black to white
From being wrong to being right
I miss you now more than before
Each day that passes more and more
Shooting star fall next to me

Who am I

Who am I?
Who is she
Is she the rebel?
Is she the slave?
Is she the smile on other faces?
Is she the hand of the lost?
Is she the eyes of the found?
Is she the statue of strength?
Is she the winning deer?
Who is she?

I was born

I was born to serve a purpose but my vision is not clear
I was born to do His work, but my ears are blocked to
hear
The vision of the Master, the vision of the One
The vision of the Father, the vision of the Son
The road is long the holes are deep
I pray the Lord my soul to keep
Keep me safe from all harm
Keep me safe keep me warm
I have chosen this life right now
We have the choice the time seems now
But what is keeping me away
I am scared, I'm afraid to say
My ignorance, my selfish ways
I don't get there, I seem to sway
Oh God, oh God, I know you're there
And of me you'll take good care
I'm stubborn like many it seems to be
I need no lock just a key
Oh God, Oh God, you know my heart is good
Oh God, oh God, you know I'll do your good

Drunk again

I kissed him, it felt like heaven
I'm drunk again
I spoke the truth, off my chest
I'm drunk again
I fell on my knees, fell on my face
I'm drunk again
I professed my love, screamed and pleaded
I'm drunk again
I climbed on the table, crawled on the chair
I'm drunk again
I forgot my inhibitions, forgot my name
I'm drunk again
I drank litres of water, litres of wine
I'm drunk again
I danced forever, I danced upright
I'm drunk again
I mumbled song words, felt like a queen
I'm drunk again
I woke up with amnesia, with a sore head
I'm hungover again
Promised not to do it again, promised myself, but
I'm drunk again

I want to tell my stories

I want to tell my stories
I want people to know
How my life has been
Which way not to go
I want to spread the news
Yell from town to town
Help people change their destinies
Help people not to frown
I want to get noticed
I want people to hear
What it's like to be alone
What it's like to fear
I want to tell my stories
Scream them loud and proud
Change the lives of people
Change the lives of crowds

Do you?

Do you want to be like me?
Popular and happy
Do you want to be like me?
Loved and cherished
Do you want to be like me?
Attractive and funny
Do you want to be like me?
Be like me
Do you want to be like me?
Sad and Lonely
Do you want to be like me?
Hateful and Bitter
Do you want to be like me?
Unforgiving and hurt
Do you want to be like me?

I can see

I can see us in the clouds
White puffy clouds
I can see us in the sand
Soft golden sand
I can see us in the waves
Roaring forgiving waves
I can see us in the leaves
Green scattered leaves
I can see us in the sky
Blue vast sky
I can see you in the light
Bright blinding light
Yes, I can see you
And you can see me
And we are together

Cane for the pain

My cane
Sweet on the lips
Bitter on the tongue
Warm in the stomach
My cane
Gone in your stomach
Thrown on your lips
Tantalising your tongue
My cane

I run

I run, run to find my tranquil place
My place far from the buildings
From buildings and statues and shadows
Shadows of my present
Shadows of my past
I run
I run to find my own shadow
My shadow of happiness
Happiness of then
Happiness of now
And as my shadow greets me
Silhouetted by the sun
I smile at the good
The good we've done and the good that's been done
For I am blessed
My shadow and me
Blessed with my family
Blessed with my friends
Many at home, some right here
Here in this place
Of buildings, statues and shadows

I pray for you

I pray for you
But sometimes forget
And blame my forgetfulness for your pain
I think of you
But sometimes think
That I am thinking of my selfishness
I pray for you

My senses

The wind blows hard today
And I can smell the sea
The birds fly high today
And I can taste the water
The clouds are still today
And I can see the waves
The air is chilly today
And I can touch the knife
The wind blows hard today
And with all my senses
The wind blows hard today
And I release a tear

Do you feel

Do you feel lonely sometimes? I do
Do you feel unheard sometimes? I do
Do you feel insane sometimes? I do
Do you feel unloved sometimes? I do
Do you feel sad sometimes? I do
Do you feel enough sometimes? I do
Do you feel tormented sometimes? I do
Do you feel? Yes, I do

I salute thee

With the wind on my back I salute thee
With the seagulls' cries in my ears I salute thee
With the sea salt taste on my tongue I salute thee
And with God's beauty in my eyes I salute thee

If you think

If you think I don't miss you every day
You'd be wrong
If you think I don't have thoughts of you
You'd be wrong
If you think I don't cry for you
You'd be wrong
If you think I don't smile at memories
You'd be wrong

If you think I'm experiencing life
You'd be right
If you think I'm meeting new friends
You'd be right
If you think I'm happy and content
You'd be right
But if you think I have battles in my head
The truth has been revealed

I can can

I can breathe
Therefore, I can smile
I can see therefore I can rejoice
I can touch therefore I can love
I can smell therefore I can appreciate
So why am I sad?

Mixed feelings

Do I enjoy the punishment of being hated?
Do I thrive on the bitterness?
Do I live for the hurt?
Do I survive on the pain?
Do I feel what I am doing?
Do I sense what's been done?
Do I?

Do I hate you? Let me count the ways

I feel insignificant when you are around
I feel no person at all
I feel insignificant when you are around
I blend in with the walls

I feel alone when you are around
I feel I have no friends
I feel alone when you are around
I have turned in to a fiend

I feel bitter when you are around
I feel it all build up
I feel bitter when you are around
I have a mind that's all mixed up

I feel hate when you are around
A feeling I cannot stand
I feel hate when you are around
I have lost my loving hand

I feel love when you are around
A feeling not for you
I feel love when you are around
A feeling once meant for you

Who is HE?

Who is he who plays God?
Who is he who takes a soul?
Who is he who sucks the life?
Who is he so hard and cold?

Who is he who plays God?
Who is he who prepares for death?
Who is he who closes the eyes?
Who is he who takes the last breath?

Who is he who plays God?
Who is he who wages war?
Who is he that causes chaos?
Who is he, no man at all

This wind

This wind
The one that blows our trouble away
That sucks the problem out of the day
This wind

This rain
The one that washes our tears away
That rinses our souls clean each day
This rain

This sun
The one that burns our stains away
That scars the good in us each day
This sun

The ocean in the distance

As I look to the ocean I see the faces of the ones I love
Caressing my eyes
Holding my face
As I look to the ocean I see memories to cherish
Thoughts of happiness, visions of splendour
As I look to the ocean I see loneliness disappear
Swallowed by the waves, hidden in the sand
As I look to the ocean I see peace rolling in
Taking my heart, consuming my soul
As I look to the ocean I see a miracle of creation
And I smile and know…
My miracles at home are looking to the ocean

Where do you go?

Where do you go to get away?
Away from all the pain
Where do you run to get away?
Away from all the hurt
Where do you hide, to hide away?
Away from all the strife
Where do you turn to turn away?
Away from the problems in your life
Where?

I remember

I remember when we joked and played
I remember when side by side we stayed
You gave me comfort you gave me peace
And every problem around us would suddenly cease
I love you now as ever before
And hope one day there will be no door
To separate us, me and you
Because I know I really love you

Ha ha

I fell but got up
I cried but wiped my tears
I laughed and spat in your face

Rough times

How deep must we dig before we burn?
How high must we fly before we fall?
I've visited the heavens
I've been to hell
I've taken the road to Tipperary
But I never say "we" I never say "us"
Always me alone
Where's the God, where's the being
The one I can't see
That one I can't see
Only the burning saint next to me

Desert dreams

The acid rain falls on my bare body
Cleansing me by opening my wounds
I am alone in this God-forsaken place
And I burn with anger and fear
I feel a shadow cover me
Only a vulture waiting for my body to rot
The positive desire I once had faded with the sunset
And I lie pathetically on my back waiting for the sand
to swallow me
My tears quench my thirst
And my eyelids close

I am

I am one speck on the globe
One care in your heart
One tear from your eye
One crease in your smile
One thought in your mind

As my hand stretches

As my hand stretches, your hand disappears
As my eyes open, your back turns
And as my heart laughs, your smile is wiped

Self-consumed

I can sit here and complain about my menial problems,
And hope voicing them makes it all better
I can sit here and cry tears of sadness for my life and
the cards I have been dealt
And hope the tears run far away
I can sit here and think thoughts of hatred,
And hope my thoughts are heard by the hated
I can sit here and write words of torture, words of pain
words of loneliness,
And hope that a hand reaches out

Or I can sit here and thank God for this minute
God for this day
And God for my life

To my valentine

You, sweet love
You, throbbing heart
You, raging soul
You, peaceful dove
You, beating sun
You, inner drug
You, red light
You, my only one

A trip to a faraway land

Sitting in my room, thinking of my choice
Blocking out the noises, listening to the voice
I'm asking if it's okay, asking if it's right
For me to leave this place, for me to take the flight
I'm told it is the greatest thing that I could ever do
But harping on what I leave behind makes me feel blue
What about my family, what about my friends?
What about the events I wish to stay to enjoy?
I guess I am just nervous about the great unknown
My life is just beginning, I should rejoice not moan
So I'll stand up and declare, that I'll make the best of it
I'll take the chance, take the leap, no longer shall I sit

In a faraway land of England

I landed here a month ago
Leaving friend and foe
A new land sat open to me
A place where dreams became reality
Where tradition is evident and histories been made
Where fundamentals and foundations have been laid
The sea has no waves, just ripples I've seen
Where nature's preserved and streets are kept clean
The sky's decorated with patterns of clouds
And streets are kept busy with festive crowds
A tourist haven with castles and forts
Landmarks, gardens, museums, ports

A friend

For a hug at my worst
Or a shoulder to cry
Making me smile
Wiping my eye
Sticking up for me
Keeping me sane
Shielding my hurt
Protecting my name
Needing my life
Showing you care
Embracing my heart
Always being there
For the smallest gestures
For your tiny ways
That I always notice
Every night and day
So let me thank you
For your friendship and love
No other human being
Could ever come above
Where I see you
Where I hold you
Where I trust you
Because I love you

A friend indeed

A friend with weed is a friend indeed
A friend like you is far and few
A friend to trust a friend to love
A friend to capture like a dove
Never to let fly far away
From my side, day after day
Keep you close, keep you near
Banish my nerves, banish my fear
A friend with strength like none I know
A friend with a heart that's selfless so
A friend to confide in when set aside
A friend to run to, escape and hide
And although we know only some of each other
I love you like family, love like a brother
And in time we'll unfold and crumble the walls
That sometimes restrict us from giving out all
So give me that time, give me the years
Give me the laughter, trust friendship and tears
Tears of love, tears of joy
Tears of friendship with this boy

On top

I hold your love above all else
You are the world to me, my sea and shore
I hold your love above all else
You are my resting place, my open door
I hold your love above all else
You are the hand that wipes my tears
I hold your love above all else
You are my safety that blocks my fears

My friend

I met this girl sometime in 1995
Personalities clicked and from that day I knew we'd be
friends for life
We started high school, my friend and me
Where we caused our teachers misery
Smoking around the corners, drinking after school
Doing all these things we thought would make us cool
We have changed schools again and again
And given our parents lots of stress and strain
But in the end we got our education
Through absence of partying and tons of patience
We have had our disagreements, and fist fights at my
house
But the friendship bond between us will never break I
doubt
And through all that has and all that's been
To me you're rated like the queen, of friendship trust
and loyalty
Being there for us… and there for me
For all the good times and bad times too
Your loving caring nature is always shining through
Your wonderful companionship has helped me through
the years
In sunshine and in shadow you have shared my hopes
and fears

So I make this pact to be your best friend now until I
die
Be there when you're up, there when you're down,
there when you laugh and cry
Again thank you for your friendship, I think of it every
day
How different life would be if you hadn't come my
way.

Our siblings

I believe siblings influence us in what we say, what we
do and how we live
They teach us, and are a part of our life we can't
represent
Siblings are the closest role models we have and often
we're their guinea pigs
They give us space when we want to fly
And crowd us when we are in need
They tell us the truth about what we're wearing,
And protect us from the bullies of life
Siblings treasure us in their boxes of gold
And lend us money when we are broke
They notify us of the latest trends and
Share with us their dreams and hopes

They involve us in their hobbies and joys
And spoil us with important information
Siblings fight with us for attention and
Often jealousy runs wild
They make us laugh, and make us cry
They make us who we are
They are our blood and flesh,
Our siblings

My sis

Thanks for all the things you do
Thanks for all the things you say
Just a big thanks to you... if I may
For being my sister, friend and pal
For being an overall excellent gal
You make me smile, laugh and cry
You make me want to live, not die
For all your love, comfort, gifts and more
For all the words of upliftment that let me soar
Without you my life would be strange
Without you my life would be deranged.

Why do we act this way?

You lie next to me, but I cannot see you
You kiss me goodnight, but I feel no affection
You hug me with your eyes, but I sense no contact
Tell me why do we act this way?

You greet me but I hear no words
You make me wanted, but I feel alone
You lend me your shoulder but I fall right through
Tell me why do we act this way?

I alone

I sit alone
I sleep alone
I breathe alone
I laugh alone
I am the fire in my heart
I am the tear in my eye
I am the grin on my face
I am the coin in my purse
I am the air I inhale
I am the fear in my soul
I am the thought in my mind
I am the am in me
I talk alone
I cry alone
I am alone
And I am thinking of you

What then?

When someone you choose, chooses someone else
What should you feel?
When someone you envy, chooses someone else to
envy
Who should I envy?
When someone takes your heart and gives it away
Have you lost it?
When someone you knew, knows more people than
you do
Do you know them?
When someone you hate, likes you more
Does that hate diminish?
When someone is selfish and so are you
Who's the better person?
When someone you care for, doesn't know you do
How can you prove it?
When all is gone, and you're standing alone
Who hears you?

Breaking up

How can I tell you without breaking your heart?
That I think we'd be better off apart
Since we've been together things have changed
Relationships different, friendships rearranged
I'm so glad you're happy, so glad you've given your heart
I'm so sad I'm about to take it apart
I don't know how to say this, without hurting you
But I know I should care about myself too
And if I'm not happy I'm not over the moon
I'd rather just be alone in my room
But pleasing you is what I seem to be doing
And I can't any more, my soul's not blooming
Don't think I don't like you, that's not it
It's just things aren't right and that's it

If

If our Lord Jesus was to return today
What would He see?
What would He say?
If our Lord Jesus came shining bright and bold
Would he see us doing exactly what He's told?
If our Lord Jesus came to see me and you
Would we be doing what we're supposed to do?
He's going to come one day soon
He's going to beam like the sun and moon
He's going take us by the hand, together to the
Promised Land
Be ready.

First mover

Who will make the first move?
I will
Who will give the first kiss?
I will
Who will say the first word?
I will
Who will reach out the first hand
I will
Who will take the first breath?
I will
Who will touch the first part?
I will
Who will see the first expression?
I will
And who will be the one to feel the shame?
I will

31 December 1999

As I write my last poem of this millennium year
I think of all the smiles and tears
For all I've done and been through this far
Memories cemented deep in my heart
As new roads lie before me, new paths to choose
Experience to gain and nothing to lose
I open my arms and welcome her gladly
Say goodbye to the past and bury it sadly

My friend in the sand

Nursery school, in the sand
That's where our friendship began
From that day, you and I
Swore a bond until we die
Primary school, we stuck together
Through days of glory and stormy weather
I broke my arms, we drank our wine,
You won the swimming and we had a good time
Then high school came and we went our ways
Separated for years, weeks and days
But reunited once again
We share together our joys and pains
As time has told our friendship is true
And after all... my best friend's you

Time is life

Time has come to say goodbye
Time has come to leave the war
Time has come to take the path
Time has come to wave you all
Life is free we're on our own
Life is free we go our ways
Life is free we take the chance
Life is free we're not in chains

History

I know it seems confusing when I don't have things to
say
But life's a mystery I try solve every day
I know I have things to tell you that I haven't said
before
But I think you know the important things and maybe a
bit more
Some stories I don't tell you not 'cause I don't feel it
right
Just some of them are stupid or may waste your time at
night
If you think that I don't trust you
I promise you I do
Sometimes words don't come out, like I always want
them to
I love you like a friend, mother, and helper too
But most of I love you just because you're you

As the sea

As the sea crashes on the sand
So my love breaks on your shoulders
The waves roll back again and again
Leaving my body dry and weak
Like rocks feeling beating water upon them
My soul is battered and bruised
Stain like watermarks
Like a seagull swooping down to catch its prey
My heart is ripped from within me
Nothing can be heard but soft groans
Alone again
Alone again the world weeps

I am human — teenage years

Don't treat me like scum, that's not what I want
Don't hate me for your pain; it's not my fault
Don't think you know me; I'm hard to understand
Don't lecture me, I probably won't listen
Don't force me, I'll just turn away
Don't choose my future, my path is my own
Don't love me, I might not appreciate it
Don't touch me, a touch could kill
Don't cry for me, your tears won't go away
Don't laugh at me, my tears stay

Can you do

Do you feel my hurt and pain?
Do you try and help in vain?
Can you see my heart that aches?
Can you sense my soul that breaks?
Do you hear my quietest call?
Do you watch my slightest fall?
Can you know when I am sad
Can you comfort if I'm sad?
Do you ever notice me?
Can you understand my plea?

Metamorphosis

As droplets fall on my hair and trickle down my neck
A slow transformation takes place
Hurt and pain flow from my heart
Into a drain of forgotten memories
I feel cleansed and pure
Nothing can steal the peace I now have
Nothing can touch my body and cause an ache
My metamorphosis is complete

A story

You become exposed to the virus that slowly infects
children
The first experience is innocent until it grips you
With claws that lock, never to let go
We don't seem to notice the dangers that wait
To gobble us up, chew us, spit us out
Leaving us scarred and confused
It's genuinely innocent
It looks attractive, an alternative route
From all the pain and discomfort, we feel
We hope or we fear
As my eyes close, pictures form in my mind
More evident than reality
My heart craves its drug
And the craving pumps through my veins
My soul builds barriers to save itself
But the strengths of the mind change the unthinkable
The desire to free my spirit is strong
While the habit is overpowering
The pain of others curses my life and
My hurt buries itself deep within
Must we die before being reborn
Must we tear, before being resewn

You act like you are in control
You put on a front
But that fades away when you're alone
And nobody can creep inside you and feel your pain
You need to help yourself out of the web you're
trapped in

You try and convince yourself, you do
But in your mind guilt covers your innocence
Like a black cloud shielding the sun
You want to blur it out, rid yourself of the pain
And the anguish, but no one's around to listen or care
The truth begins to turn and twist and you get bound
up
In a rope of lies
Your heart knows the truth but your mind turns it
against you
Like your hope turning into your worst enemy
And it grips your emotions uncontrollably

Swallowing

Look at others then pity yourself
Feel their pain, then cut your wrists
Take their poison, swallow your life

She man

She has a pocket full of empty dreams
A heart of gold that shines and beams
A place to hide, a place to seek
For when she's strong and when's she's weak
I don't know but I've been told
In this world you've got to be bold
Take my hand, we'll walk it through
You were there for me
Now I'm there for you
She spreads her wings and takes to flight
She's been torn apart and cannot fight
She wants to scream, she wants to crack
She wants to leave, but I want her back
I'll take her pain, heal her scars
Set her free, break the bars
I'm here to stay, here to care
Here to heal that open tear
Turn around you'll see me here
Arms open wide nothing to fear

When, tell me when

How many tears must they cry before you hear their
screams?
How many people must die before you read their
dreams?
How many wounds must open before you're going to
leave?
How many hearts must crack before you stop to
grieve?
How many children must drown before you pull the
plug?
How many bodies are damaged, before you take the
mug?
How many lines are sniffed before you take the glass?
How many victims are torn, before you punish his ass?
How many need to bleed, before you mend their souls?
How deep must they dig, before you cover the hole?

Home and away

The feeling of freedom has to stay
The feeling of loneliness won't go away
Being alone is fun for a while
But you need close friends to bring back that smile
Security is lost in this world apart
What keeps you going is the strength in your heart?
Soon to be reunited with the ones I love
Flying home like a runaway dove

I see

I see a lonely girl, scared to death
Afraid to reach out and take that breath
I see a fragile kid, torn apart
Given up his soul and lost his heart
I see a battered wife, bruised and scarred
She's got no place, all doors are barred
I see a giving friend who gave too much
She gave her spark and lost her touch
I see a struggling addict who can't break free
Too hurt to care, too deep to see

I want to know where do we go from here
I want to know who do we call from here
I want to know who hears our cries from here
I want to know sees our tears from here
I want to know who blocks our fears from here
I want to know who heals our hearts from here
Where do we go from here?

My star

Her face shone like the morning star
Her smile stretched like an unmarked horizon
Her voice calmed my roughest waters
Her warmth sheltered me from raging storms
Her eyes watched over me during the night
But the sickness bit her, no longer could she fight

My special You

Sometimes I sit and wonder what makes the special
you
I wonder if it's what you say, or maybe what you do
We were always close, side by side, though separated
for a while
Nothing could keep us apart for long
Apart from friendly smiles
I know I haven't been to you all you've been to me
Circumstances overruled my life like you could see
I make this past to be your best friend now until you
die
To laugh with you, watch you grow, be there if you cry
If you stumble, if you crumble, if you're going to fall
I'll be here to pick you up and protect you like a wall

You

Your presence warms the coldest air
The smallest gestures show you care
Your smile dries the wettest tears
The walls you create block my fears
Your voice comforts the most broken mind
The love you shower is so kind
Your hand calms the roughest sea
The many things you do for me
I love you yesterday, today and tomorrow
And thank you for giving me laughter from sorrow

Call on me

When life gets tough like it seems to do
Call on me like I call on you
Take your heart and let it out
Cry, scream, jump, shout
Life has its ups and downs
Stay on top and try not frown
Try to take grief with a smile
Show them you'll conquer that mile
There are those who care and don't show it
There are those who care and you know it
If you need a hand, it's waiting for you
If you need a friend, I'm here too

My song to you

To you I once believed in
To you I shed my heart
To you I told my secrets
To you I fell apart

But it hurts so deep
This cut is still wide open
But I hurt I weep
This blood is me, I'm choking

I know for you it's over
I know the past is now
I know you don't remember
My life was living hell

But it hurts, I cry
This cut is still wide open
But it hurts, oh why
This blood is me, I'm choking

To you I'll show forgiveness
To you I'll close my eyes
To you I'll say forgotten
To you who heard my cries

But it hurts me, this feeling
This cut is still wide open
But I hurt, I'm dreaming
This blood is me, I'm choking

I want to tell you bitter things
I want to make you see
I want to stretch the distance
I want to scream it's me

But it hurts it's over
This cut is still wide open
But I hurt, it's over
This blood is me, I'm choking

My song of affection

Fuzzy lines, songs that rhyme
Eyes are bloodshot all the time
Purple holes, burning coals
Places left for searching souls
Sweet smelling smoke, overdose
Rest in peace, ain't no joke

I think, I think, I think I'm wasted
And I need no affection
Think I'm wasted
And I need no attention
I think I'm wasted
And I need no sedation
I think I'm wasted
And I need no impatience

Candy flip what a trip,
Green goblins take a dip
Butch and spike, ride your bike
Prick your fingers it's just like
Ecstasy, you and me
Touch my body, can't you see

I think, I think, I think I'm wasted
And I need no affection

Think I'm wasted
And I need no attention
I think I'm wasted
And I need no sedation
I think I'm wasted
And I need no impatience

Steamy pots, yellow dots
Acting like what you're not
People envy, people stare
People try it if they dare
Now your lord, now you're bought
Web of deceit, now you're caught

I think, I think, I think I'm wasted
And I need no affection
Think I'm wasted
And I need no attention
I think I'm wasted
And I need no sedation
I think I'm wasted
And I need no impatience

Look at me

I'm looking at you, but you're staring at someone else
What's wrong with me
I'm stretching my hand, but you're hugging her
What's wrong with me
I'm pouting my heart, but you're listening to her sweet
nothings
What's wrong with me
I'm standing alone, but you turn your back
What's wrong with me
I'm ordering a drink; you pay for hers
What's wrong with me
I'm moving my body, but her moves move you
What's wrong with me
I'm dressing to kill; you're not looking at me
What's wrong with me
I speak with knowledge, you listen with ignorance
What's wrong with me
I'm a decent person; she's a tart with a bod
What's wrong with me
You want this, or do you want that
I won't change for you
You're what's wrong for me

Conviction

You lift that glass, liquid touches your lips, conviction
You smoke that joint filling your lungs, conviction
You curse that man, venom spits off your tongue,
conviction
You touch that body, hand wondering far, conviction
You close your eyes, while torment occurs, conviction
You turn you back on hungry eyes, conviction
You grasp a heart, then leave it to fade, conviction
You cause a person to cry, tears flowing down,
conviction
You lie like a snake, take a bite, conviction

Conviction, contradiction, what's going through your
head
The rate you're going; you're heading for dead...
contradiction

I disapprove

I disapprove of my reputation
I disapprove of my life
I disapprove of my loves
Will I make the perfect wife?
I disapprove of my stature
I disapprove of my joys
I disapprove of my hates
Can I play with safe toys?
I disapprove of each day
I disapprove of no friendship
I disapprove of my contacts
Who will show me the right ways?
I disapprove of my paths
I disapprove of my ways
I disapprove of my appearance
Can you just go away?
I disapprove of my figure
I disapprove of the look
I disapprove of unhappiness
I want to write a book

A song of a safe house

I see your tear-soaked eyes
Your carved in frown
Your body battered and bruised
I want to scrub it out
Make you pure
Take away your marks

So just reach out to me
Take my hand
Grab it and don't let go
Because I'm your secret place
Your lock and key
A place that no one knows

I know your clothes are torn
You have no shoes
The gravel digs in deep
I break to see you hurt
I crumble to the ground
Close my eyes and weep

So just reach out to me
Take my hand
Grab it and don't let go

Because I'm your secret place
Your lock and key
A place that no one knows

I want to know

I want to know what you see through your blurred
vision
I want to know what you feel in your golden heart
I want to know what you taste in your bitter mouth
I want to know what you drink in the desert storm
I want to know what you do in your secret moments
I want to know it all
I want to know it all
I want to know what you dream of in your nightmares
I want to know what you speak of in anger
I want to know what you touch in a moment of passion
I want to know what you think of in doubt
I want to know what you love in the morning and love
in the night
I want to know it all
I want to know it all

Cornish days

The tree
The bird
The sea
The sky
All so blessed
To the eye
The simplest nature
The tiniest sight
Makes you thankful
To the might
Of creation
Of us all
Of all creatures
Great and small
Of the sun
The moon
The stars
The rock
The blade of trampled grass
The beauty
The revel
The magnificent earth
The morning smell of true rebirth

Insomnia

Last night I fell asleep to the waves crashing
Onto a pebbled beach of rocky memories
I was awoken again and again
The beats grew stronger and echoed against my
window
And although its melody was much appreciated I
needed to block it out for my deserved sleep
But like nature unchanging and independent, I couldn't
transform the noise into my lullaby

Forgive and forget

Famous words
Release the birds
Trust again
Bitter rain
Reliance here
Perfect sphere
Swallow pride
Heart open wide
Say you're sorry
Alleviate worry
Trap of guilt
Truth is spilt
Expect return
Lesson to learn
Forgive me now
Forget somehow

So much suffering

So much pain
Suffering in vain
So much hurt
Nothing to assert
Need redemption
Failed detention
Crave apology
Pleading sorry
Released the sadness
Removed madness
Stupid mistake
Burnt at stake
Dumb move
No more to prove
Change the past
Never a mask
So much pain
Suffering in vain

Calais to Dover

As the ferry departs
A piece of me is left behind
A piece of silence
A piece of pain
As the water is moved
A part of me is left in tears
A part of struggle
A part of guilt
As the land disappears
A fragment of me is left bewildered
A fragment of confusion
A fragment of sin
And as we proceed
I am left anew
Anew with thought
Anew with wants
Anew! Anew!

This world we live in

This world we live in
Beautiful place
Filled with wonders
Thunder and grace
This world we live in
Blessing disguised
Soft on the ears
Kind on the eyes
This world we live in
Sea to shore
East to west
Heaven to core
This world we live in
Amazing creation
Diverse and alike
Nation to nation
This world we live in
Unexplainably true
A world I want to share with you

God will

God will take my burdens
God shall them bear
Because I am still weak
Because I show the tear
God will make me whole
God shall fill the void
Because I am still trapped
Because I can't avoid
God will reach the pain
God shall rip it out
Because my sadness blossoms
Because I am without
God, please help me now
God, make it go away
Because I need your help
And because I believe it when I pray

My Paris hotel room

From my Paris hotel room, all is turned into a fantasy
story tale
A Moulin Rouge of my life
An unattainable dream for others

The breeze caresses the rigid buildings
And all hope is not lost
For the season carries with it more reachable goals,
more future memories and more pleasant days

The car engines are muffled out by the local patrons,
yet stillness is still profound in this Paris hotel room

The front

I don't know if I can be this strong
I don't think I can keep this front
My heart is aching and all I can do is smile
My heart is pierced, and all I can do is praise
I don't know if I can be this brave
I don't think I can keep this mask
My heart is crippled and all I can do is laugh
My heart is scarred and all I can do is agree
I don't know if I can be this accepting
I don't think I can keep this act
My heart is torn and all I can do is joke
My heart is broken and all I can do is cry

Smile

When the world beats you, smile
When the world tackles you, smile
When the world aces you, smile
When the world spits you out, smile
When the world shoots you down, smile
When the world charges you, smile
When the world crashes your spirits, smile
When the world tempts you, smile
When the world treats you rough, smile
When the world confuses you, smile
When the world challenges you, stand proud, win and
smile

My angels

God chose angels when he sent all of you
To give direction to those who didn't have a clue
He kept your halos and stored your wings
And delivered you down to sort out things
Where there seemed no door, no open way
He lent us you to save the day
So I thank you then, I thank you now
I'll thank you every way I know how

And I know there are many who feel the same way too,
and who believe God chose angels when he sent all of
you.

Revelations

One day all will be revealed
Like the unveiling of a great work of art
One day all will be clear
Like crystal clarity of a mountain spring
One day all will be forgiven
Like an angry father opening his arms to his prodigal
son
One day all will be written
Proof of truth in a world of lies
One day things will return to the way they were
And until that day
Keep me in your heart and wait...
Until one day

Blah

I try to tell you the truth, but I can't
Try to make you see
But you are blinded
Though you try and hide it, I know
You prefer the lies to my answer

We've changed and I feel things were better when our
stubbornness was gone
We've changed and I sense no matter how I try, things
set in stone, set in sleet

I try to clear my name of the dirt
Try to polish clean all the lies
Though I try to wipe it, it's clear
Life losing you is what I fear

God in a faraway land

"Christ" a name used by many yet understood by few
This country so far away from the God, who has made
them,
God who loves them, God who needs them
Using His name in vain, like they know who He is
Sad but true

I chose

I chose to kiss you
You wanted that choice
I chose to touch you
You enjoyed that choice
I chose to feel you
You loved that choice
And now I choose to hate you
Because that you chose

I cried

I did
'Cause I can
I said
'Cause I will
I smiled
'Cause I would
I cried
'Cause I was
Sad for what I did
Glad for what I said
Content for why I smiled
And relieved for now I cried

Do I want to live just being content?

Do I want to live just being content?
No cheers for the masses
No great spending spent
Do I want to live just letting things go?
No tears of oceans
No scars to show
Do I want to live quiet and serene?
No screams of passions
No wicked dreams
Do I want to live without a word?
No strength of a lion
No grace of a bird
Do I want to live and just let live?
No defence for abuse
No opinions to give
Do I want to live just watching life go by?
No crease in my smile
No tear in my eye
Do I want to live just being content?
From this day on you'll know what was meant

To my love

For all the things I can't say
And all the things I can
I love you
For all your terrible habits
And all your adorable acts
I love you
For all your hateful possessions
And all your loveable traits
I love you
For all the gestures I can't show
And all the games I can
I love you
For all my misconceptions
And all my fallen truths
I love you
For all my broken arrows
And all my worn-out targets
I love you
And for all the words that are written
And all that's left unsaid
Nothing less
Than I love you

For all you have done

For all you have done and all you do
That make me me and make you you

It's funny when you realise when you're far away
All the different people that brighten your day
All the people that make you smile
All the ones that will walk the mile
In the flight of the birds, in the crash of the sea
In the howl of the wind, and the buzz of a bee
In the kiss of the clouds and the touch of the rain
In the warmth of the sun to melt all the pain

The little things that I'll remember forever
The small things that withstand all weather
The tiny gestures that show you care
The silent words that echo, "you're there"

So this general thanks, and "I appreciate you"
These meaningful words, "I love you"
My heart goes out, stretching my feelings
Bursting through doors, tearing off ceilings
Telling all strangers, I'm a lucky gal
For the people I know make my world real

My radio-less Nissan Micra

In my radio-less Nissan Micra, all the world stops and
everything passes by
In my radio-less Nissan Micra, I think of all my loves,
what they're doing, what they're thinking
In my radio-less Nissan Micra, I reduce my hate and
ask forgiveness for those who hate me
In my radio-less Nissan Micra, I review the past, plant
the future and drive the present
In my radio-less Nissan Micra, I thank my God, thank
creation, and thank all beings
In my radio-less Nissan Micra, I visualise my dreams,
picture my hopes and paint my fantasies,
And in my radio-less Nissan Micra, all the world stops
and everything passes by

Being an angel

Being an angel
Morning star
Being an angel
That's what you are
Being an angel
Wears no mask
Being an angel
Internal sparks
Being an angel
Say no words
Being an angel
Soar with the birds
Being an angel
Blessing on others
Being an angel
Adopted mother
Being an angel
Evening star
Being an Angel
That's what you are

A song of inspiration

I take advantage of you
Like for granted breaths of life
I forget your kind deeds
Like not remembering good health
I adore your appreciation
Like discussing selfishness
All for you...
Yeah yeah
All for you...
Take my life
Take my soul
Take my entire being
All for you...
Yeah yeah
All for you...
I throw my problems on you
Like sandstone felt pity
I use all your abilities
Like thieves in the night
I borrow your love
Like returning used goods
All for you...
Yeah yeah
All for you...
Take my life

Take my soul
Take my entire being
All for you …
Yeah yeah
All for you…

Memories of my gran

I pack you away
In unkempt drawers
Scared to remove
Vivid memories
Until a time
When pain is bliss
And dust can be swept
Without a tear
The sun would shine
And wind would blow
But now you're stored
And nothing shatters
I wore your smile
Dressed in love
Smothered in warmth
Obstacles disappeared
But clearly now
Too clearly
Heart in chains
Sunken deep
So I pack you away
Safely to rest
Until a time
When I rejoice

My heart breaks...

It crumbles
Piece by piece
Shaved off
And I smile because I do
My mind fees grey
Feels blurry and
And I smile because I do
I cry for help
Cry to my Lord
Ask the question we all ask "Why?"
I have no answer yet
But know the answer already
Why not?
The answer I dread
The answer that breaks my heart
And chips away at the confidence I have
Amidst it all I know that God my God
Is supreme and has my best interests at heart
But right here right now I feel pieces of me falling
Falling into the stream that I am supposed to envision
The stream that carries my anxiety of shallow leaves
Down the emotional stream
Drops of me
Leaking out of the patched up bottle
I have healed one area

But scratched another
This scratch is infected
Full of lies and deceit
A virus that steals hope
Steals peace
Steals the truth
But I smile because I do
I do know the ending
I do know who wins
I do know my purpose
I do know God my God holds me
Holds me as a brittle leaf
As a punctured bottle
A bleeding heart
God my God
God of the universe
Chose me
I am an example
I am a testimony
I am a soldier
And I know only the best soldiers go to war
And this war isn't against flesh, but against
Principals of darkness
And darkness has not won
My drop, my piece, my cry creates a light that's even
greater than the darkness
And this supernatural light I have been given

Will not be put out
Not today
Not ever

That man

A man, just a man
Made a life to remember
Made a print in this world
A permanent tattoo
Never to fade
A man, just a man
Human form but godly heart
Selfless soul
Giving all
Open arms
To all he met
A man, just a man
Gentle ways
Unforgettable presence
Father to many
Friend to all
Willing to help
Big or small
A man, but *not*
Just a man
An angel sent from heaven
To Earth
To see God's love
To show God's love

Shining

Shining light
The shining light that you are
The gentle spirit stretching far
The giving nature never stops
The love binding as a knot
The smile of joy on your face
The spoken words full of grace
The meaning hug of compassion
The career filled with burning passion
The countless way you have saved us all
The soft hand to guide my walk
The things above are but a few
Of the reasons
I love you

Calm down

Calm down
Calm down
When the world beats down on you
Calm down
Calm down
But soon you'll break through
There seems no easy exit
No simple defined escape
Doors are locked and bolted
Padded walls close in
Calm down
Calm down
There seem no smiling faces
No welcome stretched out
Arms are crossed and frowning
Backs turned away again
Calm down
Calm down
There seems no friendly place
The world has closed its eyes
Pain deepens in the shadows
Heart broken into pieces

Calm down
Calm down

So soak in the fading sunrays
Breathe deep the hailing wind, and
Calm down
Calm down

I think about you

I think about you all the time
Think thoughts to bring you back
But the rain keeps pouring
I think I saw you in the clouds
Images of smiles of long ago
Disappeared into spectacles
My heart aches today
I miss you and crave a hug
Voices shifted to silence
I am in quiet thoughts of yesterday
Thinking of you all the time
Wishing I could go back and change it all

Changing green

Jealousy makes you nasty
Or so the saying goes
It tears you up in too many ways
Ripping at the toes
Jealousy makes you nasty
It makes you hard and cold
It churns your insides upside down
Makes you prematurely old
Jealousy makes you nasty
You want to strangle the life
Causes you to scream and shout
Brings much grief and strife
Jealousy makes you nasty
Yes — the saying's true
But I just can't help myself
Being so jealous of you

Wakey

Wakey wakey, baby
Open up your eyes
Birds are tweeting melodies
Up in summery skies
Wakey wakey, baby
Day is fresh anew
Paths are paved golden
Especially for you
So wakey wakey, baby
Take a step outside
Mommy and Daddy waiting
To be right by your side
Wakey wakey, baby
Show us your big smile
Miracle of living
God's little child

The sounds of silence

The sounds of the children playing in the fields
The sounds of old classics spinning no yield
The sounds of birds chirping at the dawn of day
The sounds of waves crashing near far away
The sounds of silence deafening your ears
The sounds of screaming to summon all our fears
The sounds of leaves rustling with soft blows
The sounds of a heart beat picturing you grow
The miracle of conception
The miracle of birth
Of one young so innocent
Blessed to this earth

High school years

I look for truth, but only find deception
I want a friend, but have an enemy
I search for love; all they show is hate
I am good, they say I am evil

You act

You act like you are in control
You put on the front
But that fades away when you are alone
And nobody can creep inside you and feel your pain
You need to help yourself out of the web you are
trapped in

When there is someone beside you lending a hand
Offering words that say "I understand"
It's usually the truest of friends
When there's someone to turn to
Day after day
For the sunshine, laughter that they bring your way
It's usually the warmest of friends

And when someone takes time to share a warm smile,
reminisce
About things and chat for a while
It's usually the dearest of friends
You are never too busy to listen
Never hurried to care
You're always eager to offer your help
Always willing to share
And someone who loves reminiscing
And having dear friends come to mind

Is wishing for you
The best friend of all
A day that's happiest kind

A craving

As my eyes close
Pictures form in my mind
More evident than reality
My heart cries for its addiction
The craving pumps through my veins
My soul builds barriers to save itself but the
Strength of mind changes the world
The desire to be free
My spirit is strong while the habit is overpowering
The pain of others curses my life
My hurt buries itself far away
Must we die before being reborn
Must we tear before being resewn?

She took us in

She took us in
From the rain
From the pain
She tried her best
She took the test
Though days were hard
Days were dark
She made mistakes
But left her mark
Lessons learnt
Fingers burnt
Years on love instilled
From the rain
From the pain
Mothers love
Never lost
Let's celebrate
We've paid the cost

Random Thoughts of a youngster

I've been high, I've been low
I've been drunk, I've been sober
I've been a runaway, I've run home
I've snuck out, I've snuck in
I've been a raver, I've been a punk
I've travelled to far out places — some people stay
clear of
I've embarrassed myself, and taken pride in myself
I've tried most things once and some things one
hundred times
I'm never bored, and never enough
I've fallen in love, fallen out
I've written songs and cried tears to lyrics
I've been a sister and a daughter
A best friend and a girlfriend
Not yet a wife and not yet a mother

Bad on

Pain, guilt flushed out
Will this not happen to them
Voice one more time
Drug head
You want to stop you do but it's like a dream
You can't stop a dream
Square ass
Heatwaves melting
Love for me somewhere in the world
Alone forever we are
After all the beautiful trips, this
Bad on
Trust the broken glass,
Which needs precision and patience

Welcome online

My mind feels fried
and my eyes are tired
This time on stage weakens my knees
Insecurities grow in numbers
And anxiety blossoms online
But I will not water these plants
I will not be changed by my camera
I will speak proudly through my mic
And I will shift and I *will* adapt
I will deliver the message of hope
Amidst the lessons learnt
I will set the props ahead
And backdrops behind and
I will sing a song of praise
And will smile to encourage
For I am not alone in this show
And not the only lead
A world of teachers join me
My cast is all around
The audience needs me
Now more than ever
So I will rise and I will perform
I will juggle and dance and
I will be who they need me to be
Whatever that may be I will be

And they will applaud — not me
But themselves — for sitting through
For not giving up
For not leaving during the interval
and they will succeed
And they will remember this time
Where the plot changed
Where they were prepared and where they were
Equipped
To start their own show

Leaving Stonehouse

It's a sad day in Stonehouse
The clouds have covered grey
The tears have left a riverbed
When goodbyes were left to say

It's a sad day in Stonehouse
The roads are clear to go
The flowers sway in sadness
The trees have lost their glow

It's a sad day in Stonehouse
As we kiss our loves farewell
We wave a wave and blow a kiss
Treasured thoughts of tales to tell

It's a happy day in Stonehouse
Remembering time together
The memories the laughs and smiles
No matter what the weather

It's a happy day in Stonehouse
From morning through the night

As a family came together
'Til next time we unite

My dad

A man of integrity beyond compare
A man of wisdom your burdens he'll bear

A man of steel, a man of seeds
A man of Med-Lemon, a man of deeds
A man of Lindt, a man of cheese
A man of those ol' onion sammies

A man of habit and stubborn at times
But mostly real solutions he'll find

A man of talents I cannot count
A man of ideas far more paramount
A man of courage, a man of no fear
A man of value to the new frontier

A father to five who shine his love
A father we cherish far above

A husband to my mom, a provider and rock
A husband to envy around the block

A grandad, a pop, a pillar of three
A grandad of legends who they want to be

A friend and counsellor to strangers he meets
A friend of the masses no matter the street

This man is our dad who we love more than he'll know
Made in his image through him I will sow
His love, his character, his humble attire
I sit here in awe...
To be like him I aspire

Solitary sadness

Solitary sadness
Solitary peace
Quiet in the darkness
Quiet will not cease
Whispers in the corners
Whispers I can hear
Thoughts of shouting madness
Thoughts of lonely fear
Enjoy this solitary concord
Solitary still
Short lived it is
As life will soon
Overwhelm us with its will

Dig Deeper

Dig deeper
Make that abyss in your mind
Carve the dirt out of your heart
Let the river run its course
Let the water weather the rocks
Make a gully in the sand
A hole so deep you can stand
Create a path than none can break
Dig Deeper
Start anew
Block the old
Cement it up
Reinforce the closed ravine
Taste and see the Lord is good
Focus thoughts on new beginnings
Dig Deep and start fresh
Carry positive sediments
And break the banks
Create a new rush of water
A deeper flow
A permanent gorge
Dig deeper
And let go

So so

So tired but cannot sleep
So upset but cannot weep
So happy but cannot smile
So reckless stay for a while
So tearful but cannot cry
So confused wondering why
So broken but cannot mend
So soft but cannot bend
So excited but cannot shout
So confident but having doubt
So the seeds of emotions run
So this end has just begun

My heart breaks

My heart breaks
My eyes stream
Where does my help come from?
My help comes from the Lord
But I feel so alone
Broken, abused, ripped apart
Where is my help coming from?
My help comes from the Lord
But why do I feel so weak
Hopeless, fearful, sad
Where does my help come from?
My help comes from the Lord
So be still, stand firm and know that I am God
My help is yours
And you are in the palm of my hand